HOW TO BE
REALLY SMART

. . . without really trying

Other Smarties titles available:

Smarties Beautiful Beasties
Smarties Book of Wizardry
Smarties Chuckle Factory
Smarties Deadly Dinosaurs
Smarties Dinosaurs Jokes
Smarties Hairy Humans
Smarties Hilariously Funny Verse
Smarties How To Draw Cartoons
Smarties How To Make 'Em Laugh Joke Book
Smarties Joke Book
Smarties Knock Knock Jokes
Smarties Practical Jokes
Smarties Puzzle Busters
Smarties Smart Art
Smarties Smart Science
Smarties Travel Teasers
Smarties Wacky World
Smarties Wizard Joke Book

HOW TO BE
REALLY SMART
. . . without really trying

By Justin Scroggie
Illustrations by David Mostyn

Robinson Children's Books

First published in the UK by Robinson Children's Books,
an imprint of Constable & Robinson Ltd, 2002

Constable & Robinson Ltd
3 The Lanchesters
162 Fulham Palace Road
London
W6 9ER

Text © Justin Scroggie 2002
Illustrations © David Mostyn 2002

A copy of the British Library Cataloguing in Publication Data for
this title is available from the British Library.

ISBN 1 84119 461 1

Printed and bound in the EU

10 9 8 7 6 5 4 3 2 1

CONTENTS

Introduction

Did you know that ants have FIVE noses?!

You do now! But what is the point of knowing that ants have 5 noses? Or that it's impossible to sneeze with your eyes open? Because it shows that you are SMART. And SMART kids have all the fun...

AT THE ZOO...

BATS AREN'T BLIND, YOU KNOW...

WATCH ME DO AN OLLIE...

ON A SCOOTER...

WATCHING TV...

DO YOU KNOW WHERE SUPERMAN PUTS HIS CLOTHES WHEN HE CHANGES IN A PHONE BOX...?

TELEPHONE

AT CHRISTMAS

IN RUSSIA, FATHER CHRISTMAS IS CALLED GRANDFATHER FROST...!

Introduction

EATING BURGERS AND CHIPS...

TAKING MEDICINE...

MAKING EXCUSES...

Introduction

This book is brilliant for distracting teachers, amazing your friends, impressing people you fancy, insulting your enemies, delaying bedtime, bluffing, cheating at games, passing notes ...

... everything you do every day – ONLY SMARTER!

Being SMART doesn't mean you're fantastically clever. It means you SOUND like you're fantastically clever – but without all the hard work! This is the secret of a happy and successful life (don't tell your parents!).

GOOD LUCK!

Awesome Aliens

Where do aliens park their spaceships? On parking meteors! What do you call a singing planet? A pop star! Aliens are cool in books and movies, but do they EXIST?

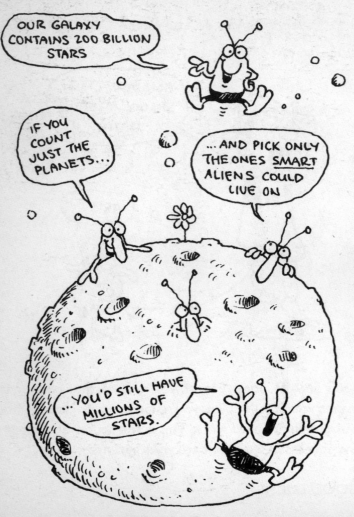

OUR GALAXY CONTAINS 200 BILLION STARS

IF YOU COUNT JUST THE PLANETS...

...AND PICK ONLY THE ONES SMART ALIENS COULD LIVE ON

...YOU'D STILL HAVE MILLIONS OF STARS.

Awesome Aliens

Scientist Frank Drake says there are so many stars in the universe, there must be aliens on SOME of them.

Awesome Aliens

But smart kids say OK – if aliens do exist, how come we've never MET any of them?

Awesome Aliens

Alligator or Crocodile?

What is a crocodile's favourite game? SNAP! What do you get if you cross an alligator with a rose? Dunno — but I wouldn't try smelling one!

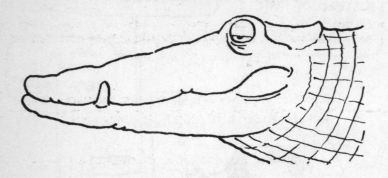

A CROCODILE has a LONG narrow snout.
ONE TOOTH shows even when his mouth is closed.
Crocodiles live in all tropical regions.

An ALLIGATOR has a BROAD flat snout.
NO TEETH show when its mouth is closed.
Alligators live in North or South America.

Alligator or Crocodile?

SNAPPY FACTS!

The best way to avoid a charging croc is to
SWERVE from side to side – they are
rubbish at changing direction!

They are the largest living reptiles. They can
grow up to 23 ft long!

Crocodiles are 'modern' dinosaurs: they first
walked on earth 90 MILLION years ago!

An alligator can eat a 4 kg chicken in a
single swallow! Who'd want to?

SNAP!!

Instant Art

Love painting? Great! But if you can't be bothered to paint anything, here are some instant ideas.

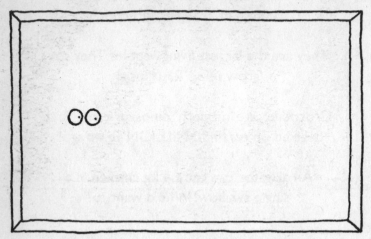

POLAR BEAR IN A SNOW STORM

BLACK CAT IN A CELLAR

Instant Art

ZEBRA AT NOON (DETAIL)

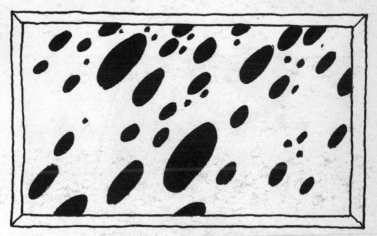

AFTER JACKSON POLLOCK
(just flick lots of different paint at it!)

All About Barbie

If all the Barbie dolls in the world were put head to toe, they would stretch round the world SEVEN times! So even if you're not a fan, you'd be smart to know about this gal!

Barbie was invented in 1959 by Ruth Handler, and named after Ruth's DAUGHTER.

Barbie's FULL name is Barbara Millicent Roberts.

Ken, Barbie's boyfriend since 1961, is named after Ruth's SON.

Barbie has 5 sisters — Skipper, Stacie, Kelly, Krissy and her TWIN, Tutti.

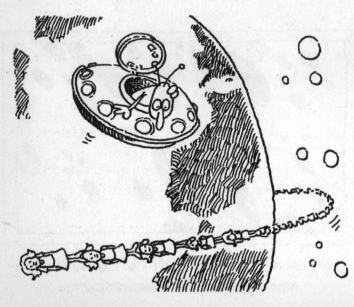

All About Barbie

Barbie has had over 40 pets including 21 dogs, 12 horses, 3 ponies, 6 cats, a parrot, chimp, panda, lion, giraffe and a zebra. Her first horse was called 'Dancer'.

Barbie was first a teenage fashion model, then College Barbie. She's had over 80 careers including Olympic swimmer, army medic, astronaut and Presidential candidate!

Barbie has represented 45 different nationalities!

Her favourite colour is pink, a unique shade called – surprise, surprise – 'Barbie Pink'.

She got her first car in 1962. It was an Austin Healy.

Doll collecting is the second most popular hobby in America (the first is stamp collecting).

Barmy Baseball Caps

What did the cap say to the scarf? You hang around while I go on ahead! Movie stars wear them. Kids in adverts wear them. Even baseball players wear them! But to look cool, be smart . . .

DO WEAR A CAP . . .
- with the peak facing forwards
- that fits your head!
- with a sporty logo on the front (a baseball team's best!)
- if you've got shortish hair
- if you're basically a kid
- if you're sporty (it *is* sports wear)

Barmy Baseball Caps

DON'T WEAR A CAP . . .

- backwards (except on a skateboard or scooter)
- that says 'one size fits all' – it doesn't
- with the name of a boring company on it
- with your ponytail sticking out like a horse
- if you're a grown-up (so s-a-a-a-d)
- if you've got big ears!

Battling Bikes

Why couldn't the bike stand up for itself? It was two-tyred! Bikes have been around for over 200 years, but the first ones were pretty uncomfortable ...

The first bike had NO handlebars and NO pedals! You moved it by pushing your feet on the ground.

Early bikes had wooden wheels – that's why they were called BONESHAKERS!

There are now 800 MILLION bikes in the world! That's two bikes for every car!

Actress Lillian Russell had a GOLD-plated bike with mother-of-pearl handlebars and spokes encrusted with diamonds and other jewels!

The TOUR DE FRANCE is the world's most famous road race for bikes.

Battling Bikes

TOP TIPS

Make sure your leg is STRAIGHT when the
pedal is at its lowest point.

Always wear BRIGHT clothes so other
people notice you!

Never cycle in the dark without LIGHTS!

Put STICKERS all over your bike – they
look great and stop people stealing it.

BIKE TYPES

Racing – for road races   BMX – for rough terrain
Mountain – for hill racing   Tandem – for two people
Tricycle – three-wheeler

Brilliant Birthdays

Everyone has a birthday once a year – even your grandma (though she's probably counting backwards)! So you have lots of chances to show just how smart you really are!

SMART QUESTION

NICE LITTLE EARNER

The song 'Happy Birthday' was actually written by Mildred and Patty Hill. Every time 'Happy Birthday' is sung in a play or film or on TV, they get paid!

Brilliant Birthdays

TWO TIMER

Queen Elizabeth II has TWO birthdays: the date she was born, and the date she was crowned Queen.

100 TODAY!

On your hundredth birthday you get a telegram from the Queen.

SMART ANSWER

SO, CLASS, WHO WAS BORN ON CHRISTMAS DAY?

ISAAC NEWTON, WORDSWORTH'S SISTER AND ANNIE LENNOX FROM THE EURYTHMICS!

Brilliant Birthdays

CLASS ACT

Did you know there's at least a 50% chance that
two people in your class have the same birthday?
Why not try it?

Brilliant Birthdays

CHANGING YOUR BIRTHDAY

Actors do it to appear younger ...
Teenagers do it to join the army early ...
People do it to avoid being April Fools ...
Americans change it to 4 July (Independence Day)
to be patriotic ...
People change it to Christmas Day to be romantic ...

Instant Book Review

Have you read *School Meals* by R. E. Volting? If you have to write down what you think about a book, just fill in the blanks!

MY BOOK REVIEW

Name of book → I found _____ easy to read because

Name of writer → _____ has a very clear style of writing.

The hero → The hero _____ really comes to life and is someone kids can identify with. I liked all the other characters except

The baddie → _____.

Name of writer → _____ is very good at describing things, and the people in the book speak in a natural way.

The story was clever, and kept me interested all the way through – I really wanted to know how it ended! The ending was sort of a surprise, but when I thought about it, I saw how it was supposed to end that way after all.

I would recommend this book to my friends.

Beautiful Book Titles

DESIGN YOUR OWN IGLOO — S.K. MOW

ROUND THE MOUNTAIN — SHEILA B. CUMMIN

HOW TO PLAY THE DRUMS

MAJOR HEADACHE

Bang on the Head — I. C. STARS

BAD HAIR DAY — DAN DRUFF

LATE AGAIN! — MISS D. BUSS

NEVER GET WET — ANNE O'RACK

TOP LASERS — RAY GUNN

WATER FEATURES — LILY POND

Bubbly Buffy

If vampires can't see their own reflections, how come their hair is always so tidy?!

Buffy Summers is just like any other girl. She has got problems with dating, school and, oh yes, slaying vampires!

She lives in Sunnydale, which is a nice place — apart from all the vampires, demons and other nasty creatures!

Her best friend is the school geek, Willow. Other current main characters include Xander, Anya, Dawn and Spike.

Sarah Michelle Gellar (Buffy) has been an actress since the age of 4. She starred in a Burger King commercial when she was just five years old.

Bubbly Buffy

VAMPIRE FACTS

The most famous vampire, Dracula, is based on a real person called Vlad Tepes who killed many Turkish people in the fifteenth century. He lived in a region of Romania called Walachia.

Bram Stoker's book *Dracula* was first published in 1897.

Bram Stoker was so ill as a child that he could not leave his bed until he was seven. He eventually got better and grew to be a strong sportsman.

Busy Burping

How dare you burp in front of your mother! I didn't know it was her turn! Even the Queen burps. She does it quietly of course – but then she's not a kid!

THE BASICS

1. Take a deep breath and hold it.
2. Close your lips and blow out your cheeks like a goldfish.
3. Sloosh the air about like there's a golf ball in your mouth.
4. Swallow all the air in one big gulp.
5. Open your mouth and B-U-U-U-R-R-P-P-P!

Busy Burping

TOP BURPING

Fizzy canned drinks are full of GAS – drink some first for a really gassy burp.

When you swallow food you also swallow a gulp of air. So when you stuff food down without breathing out between mouthfuls you often need to burp afterwards.

BURP FACTS

In Omaha, it's against the law to burp in church!

A cow makes seven litres of gas a minute – so if it doesn't burp regularly it will explode!

BELCH v BURP

What's the difference between a BELCH and a BURP?
Some say a belch is *longer* than a burp.
Some say a belch sounds *deeper* than a burp.
And others say a belch is *wetter* than a burp.

Canny Camel Humps

What do you call a camel with three humps?
Humphrey! The two best-known types of camel are the
Bactrian and the Dromedary – but what's the
difference?

A Dromedary has ONE hump,
like a 'D' on its side.

A Bactrian has TWO humps,
like a 'B' on its side.

Canny Camel Humps

HUMPY FACTS

Camels are known as SHIPS OF THE DESERT.

Camels can close their nostrils to keep sand out.

Camels can bring up their dinners and SPIT them at their enemies!

In World War II, soldiers in North Africa made cigarette lighters out of camel POO!

A camel's hump is not full of water but of FAT – which it can use as food and water when it needs to.

Camel's hair paintbrushes are actually made from SQUIRRELS' tails.

Cool Cats!

What do cats read every day? Mewspapers! What do they sleep on? Caterpillows! Cats are very cool creatures, as these SMART facts show.

BLACK cats are supposed to be lucky, except in America where *white* cats are lucky!

Tortoise-shell cats are nearly always girls!

If a cat wags its tail it is NOT happy!

White cats need to wear SUN CREAM in the summer!

Cool Cats!

We call male cats 'toms' after *The Life and Adventures of a Cat* was published in 1760 – all about a cat called Tom!

Cats have been known to predict earthquakes and thunderstorms!

Cats have an extra eyelid!

Manx cats don't have tails.

Cats can never be vegetarians!

Cool Cats!

A cat-o'-nine-tails was a whip with nine knotted thongs used for punishing sailors.

Cats sleep about 16 hours a day!

Cats like being stroked because it reminds them of being licked by their mothers when they were kittens!

Cats *don't* have nine lives! But they seem to because they're good at getting out of trouble, and nine was thought to be a lucky number.

Centipedes or Millipedes?

Why do centipedes make terrible footballers? Because they take so long to put their boots on! Centipedes and millipedes both have lots of legs, but what's the difference?

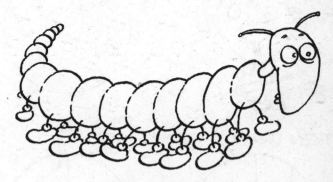

A centipede has TWO legs
on each segment of its body.

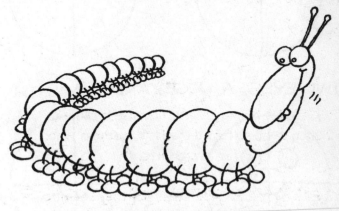

A millipede has FOUR legs
on each segment of its body.

Cartoon Capers

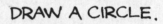

HERE'S HOW TO DRAW A HEAD.

DRAW A CIRCLE.

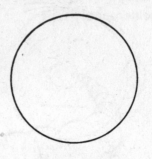

THEN DRAW A CROSS WITH

TWO EYES, A NOSE, AND A MOUTH.

Cartoon Capers

DON'T FORGET THE HAIR AND EARS.

Cartoon Capers

NOW YOU CAN DRAW A FACE, TRY AND CHANGE THE SHAPE OF THE HEAD, AND THEN DRAW DIFFERENT EXPRESSIONS.

Cartoon Capers

Champion Chess

How do you make a chess player happy? Take the knight off! Grown-ups are always impressed by kids who play chess.

HOW TO PLAY

1. There are two players — Black and White.

2. You use a board of 64 black and white squares.

3. Each player has the same set of 16 pieces.

4. You take turns to move <u>one</u> piece on the board.

5. Each piece has a <u>set</u> move (e.g. Bishops move diagonally).

6. To take an enemy's piece, land your piece on the same square.

7. To win, you must trap your enemy's King.

Champion Chess

HOW TO BLUFF

1. Let your opponent move FIRST.

2. Then COPY each of his moves.

3. Before moving your piece, stare at the board in silence.

4. After five moves, push your King over to say 'I surrender'!

5. Smile, shrug and say: 'Checkmate in eight moves'.

6. Walk away while everyone tries to work this out!

Life Cycle of Chips

Did you hear about the fight in the chip shop? Ten fish got battered! But where do chips come from?

I'm asleep in the ground ...

I get dug up and have my hair pulled out ...

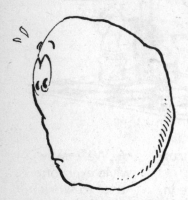

Then they peel my jacket off!

They chop me into little pieces!

Life Cycle of Chips

Thin regular slices ...   or fat chunky pieces ...

Finally, they throw my remains into boiling oil…!

SMART FACT

In America, chips are called 'fries' and crisps
are called 'chips'!
Confusing, eh?

Cracking Christmas

What happens if you eat Christmas decorations? You get Tinselitis! Better to brush your hair, smile your cheesiest smile, and say: 'Did you know that ...'

The first Christmas CARD was sent in 1844.

The ROMANS started celebrating Christmas around AD336.

Before that they used to have a week of wild parties and merry-making called the SATURNALIA! (no change there then).

Seven out of ten British dogs get Christmas presents from their owners!

Cracking Christmas

In 1975, Werner Erhard from San Francisco
sent 62,824 Christmas cards!

The TALLEST ever
Christmas tree was
53 metres high!

In Russia, Father
Christmas is known as
GRANDFATHER FROST.

Cracking Christmas

The ROYAL FAMILY give each other presents on Christmas EVE.

The town of SANTA CLAUS in Indiana receives over a MILLION bits of Christmas post every year!

In Greece, Christmas Day is on 6 January.

Ukrainians put spiders on their Christmas trees because finding a spider on Christmas Day is supposed to be lucky!

Cracking Christmas

Oliver Cromwell banned Christmas carols and parties in England between 1649 and 1660 because he thought it should be a very solemn occasion.

The day after Christmas is called Boxing Day because money for the poor was collected in boxes in churches during the festive season.

In Italy, it is a kindly old witch called La Befana who delivers presents, not Santa!

Every year since 1947 the people of Oslo have given a Christmas tree to the city of Westminster to say thank you for Britain's help to Norway during World War II.

A sweet shop owner, Tom Smith, invented crackers in 1846.

The largest real Christmas cracker was 45.72 metres long and 3.04 metres wide. It was made in Australia and was pulled in a car park on 9 November 1991.

Clever Colours

What's black and white and red all over? A penguin with sunburn! But can you remember the colours of the spectrum? Roy G. Biv doesn't need to – his name spells out all the colours in order!

ROY G. BIV

Which just happens to stand for ...

Red, **O**range, **Y**ellow, **G**reen, **B**lue, **I**ndigo and **V**iolet!

Clever Colours

COLOUR FACTS

According to Hebrew tradition, the first man,
'Adam', means 'red' or 'alive'.

Orange is the colour of love and happiness to
the Chinese and Japanese.

Green has always been associated with Spring
and new growth.

Blue symbolises peace and truth and is used
for the flag of the United Nations.

Purple has always been a royal and church
colour because in ancient cultures only
the wealthiest people like kings and
churchmen could afford the expensive purple
dyes for clothing.

Instant Crying

Crying isn't cool, but it can be SMART! Like when you're supposed to care that your brother's hurt his knee. So how do you make 'glum drops' whenever you want?

THINK ABOUT SOMETHING REALLY SAD...

RUB YOUR EYES GENTLY TO MAKE THEM SEEM RED

SNEAK TO THE BATHROOM AND WET YOUR EYES WITH WATER.

RUB YOUR NOSE HARD TO MAKE IT GO RED...

ACTORS OFTEN SNIFF AN ONION JUST BEFORE DOING A SAD SCENE

SUCK ON A VERY STRONG MINT

Instant Crying

Here are some tear-jerking ideas to get you blubbing!

Dazzling Dates

Why is history so tasty? Because it's full of dates! If you can't remember when history happened, just think of these smart rhymes!

In sixteen hundred and sixty-five
Thousands caught the plague and died.

The Great Plague spread across Europe in 1665.

At the Battle of Hastings, in 1066, William
the Norman knocked Harold for six!

William the Conqueror defeated Harold to
become the first Norman king of England.

Dazzling Dates

> In Fourteen hundred and ninety-two,
> Columbus sailed the ocean blue!

Christopher Columbus sailed across the
Atlantic to America in 1492.

> In Sixteen forty-nine it's said
> Charles the First lost his head!

In 1649, Charles I was executed and
Cromwell made England a Commonwealth.

Dazzling Dates

Here are some smart ways to remember the two World Wars:

World War I ended at...

The 11th hour of the 11th day of the 11th month of 1918

World War II began on 3 September 1939 or

3.9.39

which is much easier to remember!

Dizzy Dinosaurs

How do you take a Brontosaurus' temperature? With a very long thermometer! And here are some more smart facts about them:

'Saurus' means 'LIZARD'.
'Dinosaur' means 'Terrible Lizard'!
Brontosaurus means 'THUNDER Lizard'!

The armour-plated Stegosaurus was six metres long – but its brain was only the size of a WALNUT!

Some dinosaurs ate STONES to grind up their food inside their tummies – chickens do this today!

Dinosaurs didn't eat PEOPLE! They died out 6 million years *before* humans came on the scene!

Dizzy Dinosaurs

The Triceratops could run up to 50 kilometres an hour!

The largest dinosaur ever was the 'Seismosaurus' – it actually SHOOK the ground when it walked!

Dinosaurs did die out – but only after 165 MILLION years! Humans have only been around for about *five* million years, which is pretty weedy!

The dinosaurs may have been wiped out by the impact of a giant METEORITE that chilled the Earth.

Dizzy Dinosaurs

The Ancient Greeks thought fossils were
animals that had been magically turned to
STONE!

Some people think
there is a dinosaur
living in LOCH NESS in
Scotland!

Modern 'dinosaurs'
include crocodiles,
tortoises, cockroaches
and dragonflies!

Dashing Dogs

My dog's fond of kids — but he prefers biscuits! Every time the doorbell rings he goes into the corner — he's a Boxer!

Dogs are the most POPULAR pets in the world.

Dingoes can't BARK!

Spotty white DALMATIAN dogs were bred to run beside stage-coaches!

The most famous dog show is CRUFTS.

POODLES don't shed hair!

SAINT BERNARDs have rescued more than 2,500 people in 300 years of working in the mountains.

Dashing Dogs

DOBERMAN dogs are named after the
night watchman who developed them!

LAIKA was the first dog in space!

Labradors, Golden Retrievers and Alsatians
make the best GUIDE DOGS.

LASSIE's TV series ran for 17 years.

Movie dog RIN TIN TIN, had his
own valet, chef, car and chauffeur!

CARTOON dogs include Scooby Doo, Lady,
Pluto, Spike and Gnasher.

African or Indian Elephant?

What's the DIFFERENCE between an African and an Indian elephant? About 3,000 miles! OK, what *else* is different?

An AFRICAN elephant is
dark grey with a hollowed back.
Big tusks and ears.
Two knobs on tip of its trunk.

An INDIAN elephant is
light grey and smaller with an arched back.
Small tusks and ears.
One knob on the tip of its trunk.

African or Indian Elephant?

ELEFACTS!

Elephants are the only animals that can't JUMP.

Elephants are the only animals with four knees!

Elephants are often called JUMBO after a famous elephant (called Jumbo!) that used to belong to Barnum's Circus and later lived at London Zoo.

JUMBO JETS are named after Jumbo elephants because they are so big!

African elephants STAND UP for 30–40 years at a time!

How To Pass Exams

Roses are red, Violets are blue; I copied your test, and failed too! So we asked the people who mark exams for their TOP TIPS:

READ THE INSTRUCTIONS

Don't start writing madly and skip any instructions at the top – like how many questions you're supposed to answer!

PLAN YOUR ANSWERS

Choose your best questions and write them out on scrap paper. While you're doing one question, your brain will think about the others. Jot these thoughts down on the scrap paper to use later – this really works!

How To Pass Exams

ANSWER THE QUESTION

It's easy to see a familiar word and write down everything you know about it! But it's much better to simply ANSWER the question.

WATCH THE CLOCK

Make sure you have time to answer EVERY question. Divide the time you're allowed by the number of questions set. Spend ONLY that time answering each question – or you won't finish!

WRITE CLEARLY

Not everyone writes beautifully. But if the examiner can't read what you've written, you lose marks. It's as simple as that.

Excellent Excuses

WHY WERE YOU LATE FOR SCHOOL?

BECAUSE YOU ALWAYS RING THE BELL BEFORE I GET THERE.

I WAS DREAMING ABOUT THE WORLD CUP FINAL AND IT WENT INTO EXTRA TIME!

I HAD TO FEED THE ANIMALS BEFORE SCHOOL – AND I JUST GOT AN ANT FARM!

I SQUEEZED OUT TOO MUCH TOOTHPASTE AND IT TOOK AGES TO GET IT BACK IN THE TUBE!

I HAD TO TAKE MY BIRTHDAY SUIT TO THE CLEANERS!

I MUST HAVE OVER-WASHED!

Excellent Excuses

WHY HAVEN'T YOU DONE YOUR HOMEWORK?

THE DOG ATE IT!

'JOHNNY WOZ TOO ILL TO DOO HIS HOMWURK LAST NITE' – SIGNED 'MY DAD'!

IT'S WRONG TO PUNISH PEOPLE FOR SOMETHING THEY HAVEN'T DONE!

I MADE A PAPER PLANE OUT OF IT – AND IT FLEW OUT OF THE WINDOW!

WE RAN OUT OF LOO PAPER THIS MORNING!

Excellent Excuses

WHY IS YOUR SCHOOL REPORT SO BAD?

MY TEACHER DOESN'T LIKE ME BECAUSE I'M SO CLEVER!

OUR GEOGRAPHY TEACHER KEEPS TALKING ABOUT PLACES I'VE NEVER BEEN TO!

BECAUSE MY TEACHER CAN'T READ DAD'S HANDWRITING!

MY MATHS TEACHER DOES LIKE ME - SHE PUTS KISSES BESIDE ALL MY SUMS!

IT'S NOT MY FAULT I DON'T SIT NEXT TO 'BRAINY' BROWN ANY MORE!

What You Didn't Know About Famous People

Lucky kids who lived a hundred years ago had a lot less history to learn! But all those grown-ups who fought battles or ruled countries also did other things it would be smart to mention!

British Prime Minister, Winston Churchill, was born in a LADIES' cloakroom!

Winston had two beds. When he couldn't get to sleep in one, he tried the other!

Explorer, Sir Walter Raleigh, brought tobacco and the potato to England!

After Sir Walter died, his wife kept his head in a bag beside her for the next 29 years!

What You Didn't Know About Famous People

Michaelangelo, Johann Sebastian Bach and Leonardo da Vinci were all LEFT-HANDED.

Charles Darwin had a stammer.

Florence Nightingale used to keep a small OWL in her pocket – like Harry Potter!

TU-WIT
TU-WOOOOO

Admiral Lord Nelson used to get SEASICK!

What You Didn't Know About Famous People

Neil Armstrong's boots were size 9¹/₂ on the MOON.

Einstein didn't wear SOCKS!

Beethoven wrote much of his most famous music after he went DEAF! (His last words were: 'I shall hear in heaven.')

Alfred Nobel, founder of the Nobel Peace Prize, invented DYNAMITE!

Instant Father's Day Card

Smart kids *never* forget Father's Day (if they want pocket money!). To make an instant card, fold a piece of paper. Copy the picture below onto the FRONT and write the verse opposite INSIDE!

FATHER'S DAY

Instant Father's Day Card

To my Dad,

This is my Dad
He's not TOO bad
But compared to the rest
He's the Best!

Lots of Love _____

Broken Finger Trick

If you broke four fingers in an accident, what would you have? No more piano lessons! Here's a sneaky trick that will make your friends and family jump!

1. Make an 'O' with your left thumb and forefinger.

2. Put the 'O' over your right thumb.

3. Click your left thumb and fingers together.

4. At the same moment, twist your right hand.

5. People will think you've 'broken' your right thumb!

Fancy Football

Why did the football coach flood the pitch? He wanted to bring on his sub! Lots of kids DON'T know how to play football (yes, it's true!) so here are the basics.

1. There are two teams, each with 11 players.

2. Players move a ball round a pitch using anything except arms and hands.

3. The aim is to put the ball in the other team's 'goal'.

4. Each team plays towards the other's goal.

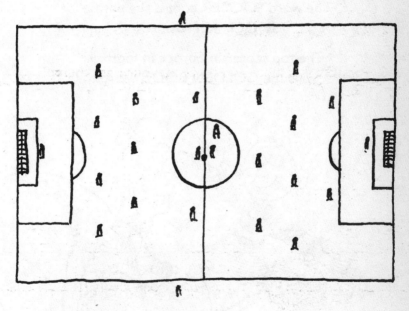

5. If you kick the ball off the pitch, the other team throws it back in.

6. Only goalkeepers can pick up the ball.

7. Team with most goals after 90 minutes wins!

Fancy Football

FACTS TO THROW IN

George Best was the first player to
be given a RED CARD and sent off.

In 1895 the FA Cup was stolen
from a shop in Birmingham.

Manchester United used to
be called Newton Heath.

The word SOCCER comes the phrase
as<u>SOC</u>iation Football.

The top scorer in European football
wins the GOLDEN BOOT award.

POK!!!

Fancy Football

TOP TIPS

The smart way to practise heading is with balloons – because the 'ball' moves slowly, you can work on your technique!

The smart way to make your new boots fit quickly is to wear them in the bath!

The smart way to keep goal is to hang your arms loosely at your sides and move sideways along the line like a crab!

The smart way to clean those white lines on your boots is with toothpaste!

The smart way to throw in is to stand sideways and turn forwards as you throw – it gives you extra power.

Instant French

Why did the cow say 'Baaa'? He was learning a foreign language! But you don't have to. Simply read out the (weird) sentences below and you'll be speaking French – sort of.

KELL URGH! AY TEEL?
What time is it?

JAY FAM!
I'm starving!

PLUE DAY FREETS, SEE VOO PLAY
More chips, please!

MA SIR AYOON BABOO EEN
My sister is a baboon.

DONNAY MWAR LARJON DEPOSH
Give me pocket money.

Instant French

JUR DETEST LECKOLL
I hate school!

PARLAY VOO FRONSAY?
Do you speak French?

OO AY LA TELLAYCOM ON?
Where is the TV remote control?

PARLAY ALLAMAN PARSKUR
LA VEE SARGE NECOOTAY PAH!
Talk to the hand, 'cos the face ain't listening!

JUR TAME – PAAAR!
I love you – not!

Frog or Toad?

What's a frog's favourite drink? Croaka Cola! But what's the DIFFERENCE between a frog and a toad?

A FROG has smooth damp skin, and long narrow head.
Slim body, and long legs it hops around with.
Frogspawn in clusters.

A TOAD has warty dry skin and short wide head.
Squat body, and short legs it hops, walks and runs with.
Toad spawn in ribbons.

Frog or Toad?

WARTY FACTS!

French people eat frogs' LEGS
as a special treat!

Some frogs and toads have POISON
on their backs that can kill in seconds.

The CANE toad of Australia
can be over half a metre long!

Toad-in-the-hole is a dish of
SAUSAGES cooked in batter!

FLYING frogs glide
between trees using
webbing between their
toes and fingers.

WITCHES keep toads as
their 'familiars' (spirits in
animal form).

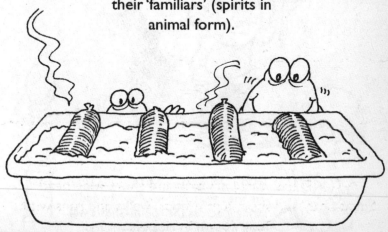

Ghoulish Ghost-Busting

Is your home or school haunted? Maybe it's just a noisy pipe or a practical joke. Maybe it isn't! You need our ghost-busting kit.

MASKING TAPE
Seal the windows and mark position of objects (in case they move!)

THERMOMETER
Are there cold spots in the room?

COTTON REEL & KEYS
Tie the keys to a line of cotton and string it across the room. Ghosts will walk through it – hoaxers will trip and make a noise!

Ghoulish Ghost-Busting

CHALK AND BLACK PAPER
Does a ghost want to leave a message?

FLOUR
Scatter flour on the floor: Ghosts don't leave footprints – hoaxers do! (ask your mum first!)

TAPE RECORDER
If you have a recorder – or can borrow one – leave it on in the room and see if you pick up any spooky sounds.

NOTEBOOK
Keep notes of what you find: sounds smells, temperature, draughts. Is there a normal explanation?

Cool Ways To Say Goodbye

Do you like getting the last word? Well, 'Goodbye' IS the last word! And there are lots of ways of saying it:

ENGLISH
Missing you already!
Catch you later.
Don't go changin' now!
Don't be a stranger.
See you later, alligator.
TTFN (Ta Ta For Now)

TEXT   CU L8R

ITALIAN   Ciao ('chow')

JAPANESE   Sayonara

SOOTY   Wave your thumb

HAWAIIAN   Aloha (also means hello!)

FRENCH   Au revoir ('oh revwar')

TA TA!

Great Graffiti!

I WASN'T HERE!

Is there intelligent life on earth?
Yes - but I'm only visiting

I USED TO BE INDECISIVE BUT NOW I'M NOT SURE

KILROY WAS HERE!

THERE'S NO FUTURE IN TIME TRAVEL!

DO POCKET CALCULATORS COUNT YOUR POCKETS?

I ALWAYS FINISH WHAT I STA

How To Win Hangman

HOW TO PLAY

Think of a word (or phrase). Now draw a line of blank spaces — one space for each letter in the word.

e.g.

———— ——— ——— ——— ——— ————

If your opponent calls out a letter that's in your word, you fill in the blank space. If the letter called out is <u>not</u> in your word, you fill in one part of a drawing of a 'hanging man'.

e.g.

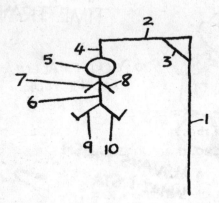

If your opponent guesses your word before the man is 'hanged', you lose. If you finish 'hanging' the man, you win!

How To Win Hangman

HOW TO WIN

The smart way to guess the right letters is to know which letters are most likely to be in the word. Here are some tips:

- The letters you find most often are: *a, s, i, n, t, o, e, r*

- The letter used most often is *'e'*

- Words rarely end with *a, c, i, j, o, q, u, v*

- Almost every word has a vowel or a *'y'*

- The letters you most often find side-by-side are:
  th, he, an, in, er

- *'q'* is followed by *'u'*

- In a phrase, the short words are usually one of these:
  the, of, and, to, a, in, that, is, I

- A blank on its own is usually *a* or *i*

And if it's your turn to pick the word, choose ones that break as many of these rules as you can!

Hot Hamburgers

Next time you're tucking in to this fast food favourite, why not come out with a few of the smart facts below!

- THERE'S NO 'HAM' IN HAMBURGERS. THEY WERE MADE POPULAR BY SAILORS FROM THE PORT OF 'HAMBURG'.

THE McDONALDS EMPIRE WAS BUILT BY RAY KROC. THERE'S ACTUALLY A HAMBURGER UNIVERSITY IN CHICAGO! THE BIG MAC WAS INVENTED BY JIM DELLIGATTI OF PITTSBURGH. FILLINGS INCLUDE MUSTARD, MAYO, ONION, TOMATO AND GHERKIN.

ONE OF THE LARGEST HAMBURGERS EVER COOKED WAS IN AUSTRALIA IN 1972. IT CONTAINED 173 lbs OF BEEF AND WAS 1.358 METRES WIDE!

All About Harry Potter

How does Harry Potter drink tea? Using a cup and sorcerer! If you haven't caught up with Harry's adventures (have you been on the moon or something?), then read on ...

Harry lives with his Aunt Petunia, Uncle Vernon and cousin Dudley Dursley at 4 Privet Drive, Little Whinging.

The Dursleys are 'muggles' – non magic people – but Harry is really a Wizard!

To wizards, Harry is famous for the scar on his forehead. Dark wizard Lord Voldermort killed Harry's parents but couldn't kill him. He lost his powers and Harry got his scar.

An owl brings Harry a letter inviting him to Hogwarts School of Witchcraft and Wizardry.

Harry travels there from Platform 9¾ at Kings Cross station, aboard the Hogwarts Express.

All About Harry Potter

At Hogwarts, the Sorting Hat puts Harry into Gryffindor House, which has a resident ghost called 'Nearly Headless Nick'.

Harry's best friends are Ron Weasley, megabright Hermione Granger and Hogwarts' gamekeeper and giant Hagrid.

His arch enemies are Draco Malfoy, Vincent Crabbe and Gregory Goyle.

Hagrid buys Harry his very own owl – Hedwig.

Hagrid has a horrible three-headed dog called Fluffy!

All About Harry Potter

Harry learns to play a flying ball game called Quidditch
and gets his own fantastic broom – a *Nimbus 2000*.
He is the youngest Quidditch player in 100 years!

His teachers include Albus Dumbledore, Minerva
McGonagall, Madame Hooch and the mysterious
Severus Snape.

The Wizard newspaper is called *The Daily Prophet*
and the Wizard bank is called 'Gringotts'.

Author J.K. Rowling wrote *Harry Potter & the
Philosopher's Stone* on scraps of paper in her
brother's café.

Heroic Hobbits

These wonderful creatures appear in *The Hobbit* and *The Lord of the Rings*, and if you haven't met them yet, it's time you did!

HOBBITS are short hairy human-like creatures with pointed ears and furry feet!

They were imagined by John TOLKIEN, a professor at Oxford.

Tolkien wrote a story for his children about BILBO BAGGINS and his adventures in a world called Middle Earth.

The first line – 'In a hole in the ground there lived a hobbit' – just popped into his head one day when he was BORED!

Heroic Hobbits

The Lord of the Rings is a bigger book about Bilbo's nephew FRODO and his friend Sam Gamgee who battle against Sauron the Black.

Bilbo took a RING of power from the slimy Gollum. Frodo must travel to Mordor, Sauron's scary kingdom, to destroy the Ring for ever.

Bilbo and Frodo are helped by GANDALF the White Wizard, who is very good at fireworks!

Over 50 MILLION copies of *The Lord of the Rings* have been sold, in 27 different languages!

Hip Hellos!

What do you say to a three-headed monster? Hello, Hello, Hello! Here are some smarter ways to greet people:

ENGLISH	Hi There! How ya doing?
AUSTRALIAN	G'day! Hello possums.
GAME SHOW	Nice to see you, to see you nice!
TEXT	LO How RU?
FLOWERPOT MAN	Flob a dob
LATIN	Ave! ('ah vay')
POLICE	Evenin' all.
ITALIAN	Bon giorno ('Bon Jaw No')
HAWAIIAN	Aloha (also means goodbye!)
FRENCH	Bonjour ('Bon Jaw')
TELETUBBY	Eh-oh

Instant Illness

Don't fancy school today? Want to get out of P.E. lessons or that boring maths test? Help is at hand with our handy instant illness guide.

Instant Illness

If you're asked to name your illness, here are a few useful replies!

I have a mild viral infection of my mucous membranes.
—
I HAVE A SLIGHT COLD

I have acute clinophobia
—
I HATE GOING TO BED

I am suffering from borborygmus (bore-bore-igg-muss)
MY TUMMY'S RUMBLING!

I have mild nasopharyngitis (nasso-farin-jie-tiss)
I HAVE A SLIGHT COLD!

Instant Illness

We all need SICK NOTES sometimes – but mums and dads don't always have time to write them. Here's an instant version – just choose the words that apply to you.

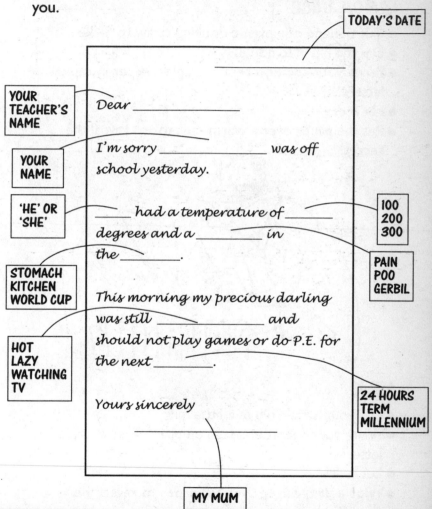

TODAY'S DATE

YOUR TEACHER'S NAME

Dear _____

YOUR NAME

I'm sorry _____ was off school yesterday.

'HE' OR 'SHE'

_____ had a temperature of _____ degrees and a _____ in the _____.

100 200 300

STOMACH KITCHEN WORLD CUP

PAIN POO GERBIL

This morning my precious darling was still _____ and should not play games or do P.E. for the next _____.

HOT LAZY WATCHING TV

24 HOURS TERM MILLENNIUM

Yours sincerely

_____

MY MUM

Invisible Ink

Do you like invisible ink? Really? What's your favourite colour? Invisible ink is very easy to make.

LEMON JUICE

- Cut the end of a plastic drinking straw to make a nib
- Dip the nib in lemon juice
- Write your secret message on plain paper in capital letters
- Let it dry
- Put the paper over a warm radiator to reveal the secret!

MILK

- Dip your 'straw' nib in a little milk
- Write your secret message on plain paper in capital letters
- Let it dry
- Wipe a dirty finger over the paper to reveal the secret!

Impressive Impersonation

Do you like copying your friends or favourite TV star? Here are some top tips.

I'M FROM BIRMINGHAM

THE VOICE

Choose victims with unusual voices – people with regional accents, who speak slowly or fast, with high or deep voices. Professionals record voices on tape to listen to over and over again – practice is everything.

WHAT THEY SAY

People have things they *always* say. TV stars have 'catchphrases' like 'I'm from Birmingham' or 'Eh-oh!'. You might know someone who keeps saying 'know what I mean? or 'wicked!' or 'like'.

Impressive Impersonation

MANNERISMS

Do your victims wave their arms when they talk?
Do they smile, put their heads on one side, or
walk in a funny way? Watch them closely and see
which of their habits you can copy.

PROPS

A 'prop' helps your audience 'see' who you're
impersonating. This might be some clothing, like
a hat or a scarf, or a guitar or a pair of glasses
or a painted moustache. Keep it simple.

Impressive Impersonation

TELL THEM!

Don't ask people to guess who you're 'doing' –
in case they can't! Tell people in advance, and
then let them pick up all the clues – the voice,
the catchphrase, the walk, the prop, etc.

MARILYN MONROE

LASTLY . . .

If all else fails, put your right hand up, palm
facing the audience and wave your thumb about.
When they ask what you're doing say
'Look! It's Sooty – in the nude!'

Insolent Insults

It's not always smart to insult people — but sometimes you've just got to! So make it a good one!

Insolent Insults

YOU LOOK LIKE A MILLION DOLLARS —ALL GREEN AND WRINKLED.

SHE'S SO DUMB— WHEN I SAID: 'LOOK, THERE'S A DEAD BIRD,' SHE LOOKED <u>UP</u>.

IS THAT YOUR HAIR— OR ARE YOUR BRAINS UNRAVELLING?

YOUR CHEEKS ARE LIKE FLOWERS — CAULIFLOWERS.

Juicy James Bond

'The name's Bond. James Bond.' Yes, he's the coolest secret agent ever. But what are HIS secrets?

FOR SMART EYES ONLY

NAME: <u>JAMES BOND</u>

CREATED BY: IAN FLEMING, EX-INTELLIGENCE OFFICER

WORKS FOR: HER MAJESTY'S SECRET SERVICE

CODE NAME: 007 – 'OO' = LICENSED TO KILL

BOSS: 'M'

COVER JOB: 'UNIVERSAL IMPORT AND EXPORT'

FIRST SEEN: <u>BOOK</u> – *CASINO ROYALE*

<u>MOVIE</u> – *DOCTOR NO* IN 1962

MARRIED: TO TRACY IN *ON HIS MAJESTY'S SECRET SERVICE*

FAMILY: ELDER BROTHER CALLED HENRY

MOTTO: 'THE WORLD IS NOT ENOUGH'

LIKES: VODKA MARTINIS [SHAKEN NOT STIRRED]

DISLIKES: TEA (CALLS IT 'A CUP OF MUD')

ENEMIES: SMERSH, SPECTRE, MR BIG, SCARAMANGA, ERNST BLOFELD, ROSA KLEBB ETC.

GADGETS: SUPPLED BY 'Q' – MAJOR BOOTHROYD

CIA FRIEND: FELIX LEITER

Juicy James Bond

EGGS! SHCRAMBLED EGGS!

FLEMING FACTS

- Named Bond after a bird-watching friend in Jamaica
- Wrote all the Bond books on a gold typewriter!
- *Golden Eye* was named after Fleming's house!
- Also wrote *Chitty Chitty Bang Bang*!
- Fleming said the only thing he and Bond had in common was they both enjoyed scrambled eggs!

TOP BOND ACTORS

Sean Connery
George Lazenby
David Niven
Roger Moore
Timothy Dalton
Pierce Brosnan

'Q' FACTS

Desmond Llewellyn who played 'Q' appeared in more Bond movies than any other actor. He bowed out in *The World is Not Enough*, replaced by actor John Cleese.

Just Jeans

What has a hundred pairs of legs but can't walk? Fifty pairs of jeans!

THE INVENTION OF JEANS

Gold was found in California. People rushed to dig it up and and get RICH.

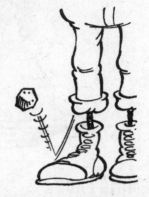

The gold NUGGETS made holes in the miners' trouser pockets!

Levi Strauss made them strong trousers from DENIM material, with copper RIVETS to stop them tearing.

Levi Strauss' company still sells Levi jeans today, as do lots of other people!

Just Jeans

WHY ARE THEY CALLED JEANS?

Denim trousers are also made from a tough
cloth called JEAN Fustian.

WHO WEARS THEM?

Because jeans were so strong, they were
worn by COWBOYS in the Wild West and
LUMBERJACKS in Canada.

In the 1950s, jeans and T-shirts became the
TEENAGE fashion.

In the 1990s, RIPPED jeans were essential
to the GRUNGE look!

Nowadays, everyone wears jeans –
except golfers, who think loud checked
trousers are 'smarter'. Go figure ...

How To Tell Jokes

There's nothing cooler than telling jokes well. And there's nothing worse than telling jokes badly! Here are some tips from the professionals.

CHOOSE YOUR AUDIENCE
Tell the right joke to the right person!

LEARN IT!
Make sure you know the joke REALLY well!

PRACTISE!
Practice stops you laughing at your OWN jokes.

How To Tell Jokes

CHOOSE YOUR MOMENT
If people aren't in the mood they won't find
ANY joke funny.

TIMING
WAIT till people are listening, then tell the joke
clearly. Don't leave people time to guess the
answer or shout it out.

RIDE THE WAVE
Once people START laughing they want to carry on.
Tell another joke DURING the laughter – this is
called 'riding the wave'.

Jazzy Juggling

Juggling takes practice! But it is a skill you can use anywhere to impress everybody.

1. Practise throwing just one ball from hand to hand with your hands about waist level. Then you simply throw it to the other hand in an arc about eye level.

2. Now try two. This is where people start to freak out. You must throw both balls UP. One up, and ...

3 ... *before* you catch it, toss the other one up. The balls must be staggered. Don't even think of using three balls until you have mastered this!

Jazzy Juggling

4. Now try three. Start with two in one hand and one in the other. Throw one up...

5. Before you catch that one, toss another one up (just like you were juggling two) ...and so on.

6. Now practise, practise, **practise!**

SMART FACT
Enrico Rastelli could juggle with TEN balls!

Crazy Kings & Queens

Where are English kings usually crowned? On the head! What is the first thing Henry VIII did when he came to the throne? He sat down! And now for more amazing royal stories ...

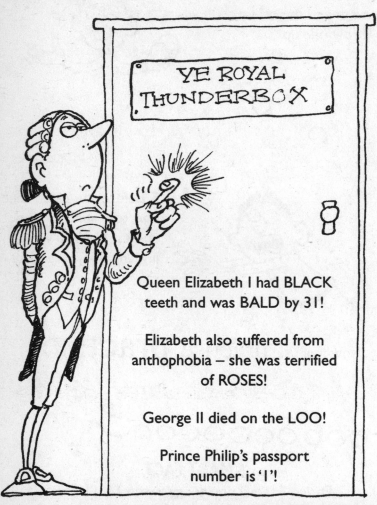

YE ROYAL THUNDERBOX

Queen Elizabeth I had BLACK teeth and was BALD by 31!

Elizabeth also suffered from anthophobia – she was terrified of ROSES!

George II died on the LOO!

Prince Philip's passport number is '1'!

Crazy Kings & Queens

Queen Elizabeth II's nickname
in the family is LILIBET!

Queen Anne was so FAT she
was buried in a square coffin!

George V kept his clocks half-an-
hour fast so he wouldn't be
LATE!

Edward VII's nickname
was TUM-TUM!

Crazy Kings & Queens

Victoria's first act on becoming
Queen was to command that all
her dogs be given a hot BATH ...
she had nearly 80 of them!

William the Conqueror's wife, Matilda,
was only 4 foot 2 inches high
– the SHORTEST queen ever.

Louis XIX was only King of France
from breakfast to teatime on
2 August 1830!

Charles I had a stammer – until his
head was chopped off!

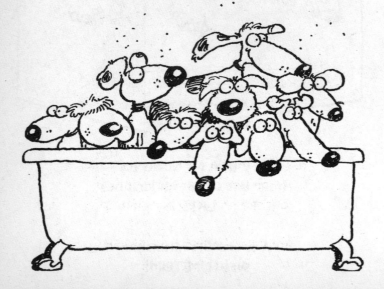

Crazy Kings & Queens

To avoid being bothered by insects,
Pepi II of Ancient Egypt kept slaves
covered in HONEY!

As a girl, Queen Victoria had HOLLY
put on her throat during meals
to make her keep her chin up!

Anne Boleyn had six FINGERS
on her left hand!

How To Spot When Someone's Lying

I told him I couldn't stop telling lies — but he didn't believe me! When we tell lies, our bodies know it isn't smart so they give off 'signals'. Here are a few — maybe they sound familiar!

YOUR HEART BEATS FASTER

YOU BREATHE FASTER

YOU START TO SWEAT

YOU GO RED

How To Spot When Someone's Lying

YOUR PUPILS
GET BIGGER!

YOU DON'T LOOK
DIRECTLY AT PEOPLE

RAT-A-TAPPITY-
TAP-TAP!!!

YOU MAY TAP YOUR FOOT OR FINGERS

How To Win Mazes

How do you find a rabbit lost in a maze? Go in and make a noise like a carrot! Want to beat the Maze Masters? The safest way of getting out of a maze is this.

HOW TO WIN

When you go in, put your HAND on one wall — left or right side, it doesn't matter as long as you KEEP your hand on the same wall ALL the time. It isn't the quickest route — but you will get out in the end!

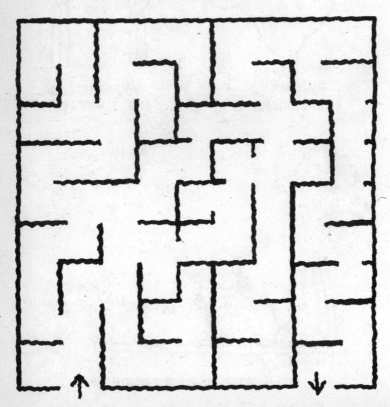

How To Win Mazes

A-MAZE-ING FACTS

The most famous maze in history is
the Labyrinth. Inside it lived the
MINOTAUR – half-man, half-bull –
who ate people who got lost!

THESEUS killed the Minotaur and
found his way out by following a ball
of STRING he had unravelled on
his way in!

Hampton Court Palace in London has
a famous HEDGE Maze.

Labyrinthus in France is a fantastic
theme park of Mazes. Every year they
GROW a huge corn maze!

Cool Ways To Take Medicine

Taking medicine is horrible – but it's worse being ill. It's not very cool to make a fuss (we all do!). But there is a SMART way to take medicine.

Suck a mint first – it takes the taste away!

Hold your nose so you don't smell it!

Have a sweet handy – it's a treat and it takes away the taste.

Clean your teeth first – the cold water and mint hides the taste!

Suck an ice cube just before taking it.

* Remember – never take medicine unless a grown-up is with you.

Monkey or Ape?

What's the DIFFERENCE between a monkey and an ape?

Monkeys are SMALLER.
Their LEGS are as long (or longer) than their arms.
They have long TAILS.

Apes are usually LARGER.
An ape's ARMS are longer than its legs.
Apes don't have much of a TAIL.

Mysterious Mind-Reading

Did you hear about the stupid idiot who went to a Mind Reader? He got his money back! Here's a smart trick to show how good YOUR mind-reading skills are.

Put a handful of different coins on a table.

Turn your back and ask a friend to pick up *one* coin.

Tell the friend to hold the coin *tightly* and think about it for 30 seconds.

Tell your friend to put it down again and muddle up the coins.

Mysterious Mind-Reading

Pick up the coins one at a time, and amaze your friend by picking out the one s/he chose!

Now touch all the coins and pick out the one s/he thought about!

How did you do it? Simple: the coin your friend held will be the *warmest*!

SMART TIP

To be *really* smart, cool the coins down first in the fridge.

How To Remember Months

Which month has 28 days? All of them! Here are two SMART ways to remember the number of days in a month.

1. THE KNUCKLE METHOD

Clench your fist so that your knuckles stand out. Then count through the months like this:

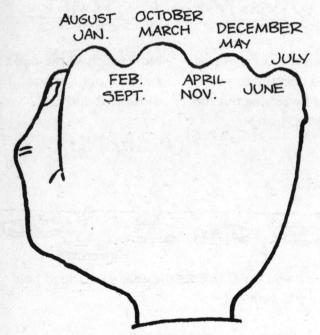

AUGUST JAN. OCTOBER MARCH DECEMBER MAY JULY

FEB. SEPT. APRIL NOV. JUNE

If a month is on TOP of a knuckle it has 31 days.
If it is BETWEEN two knuckles it has 30 days.
Except for February . . .

How To Remember Months

2. THE POEM METHOD

Memorise this simple poem:

30 days in September,
April, June and November.

All the rest have 31,
Except for February alone.

This has 28 days a year,
And 29 in a Leap Year.

All About the Moon

Two astronauts went to a party on the moon, but they left after a few minutes. It had no atmosphere!

The moon is 376,275 km away.

People used to say the moon was made of CHEESE because it is round, yellow and full of holes.

Have you noticed that a FULL moon seems to have a jolly FACE?

All About the Moon

The first man on the moon was American astronaut NEIL ARMSTRONG.

Armstrong's FIRST words were:

Armstrong's SECOND words were:

Armstrong's first MEAL on the moon was
roast turkey (from a foil packet).

Twelve men have walked on the moon ... so far!

All About the Moon

On the moon, an earthquake is called . . .
a MOONQUAKE! There are
about 3,000 of them every year.

In the seventeenth century Sir Paul Neale
announced that he had discovered
an ELEPHANT in the moon.
It turned out that a mouse had
crept into his telescope!

If you stood on the moon you
would be six times LIGHTER!
Good for diets!

Because the moon has no wind or water,
the FOOTPRINTS made by the Apollo
astronauts will probably still be there
in 10 million years' time!

The moon, like space, is completely SILENT.
There is no air to carry sound from one
place to another, so noises cannot be heard.
So much for all those explosions in *Star Trek*!

The moon causes the TIDES on Earth
because its gravity pulls our seas towards it.

All About the Moon

Instant Mother's Day Card

Smart kids never forget Mother's Day! To make an instant Mother's Day card, fold a piece of paper. Now copy the picture below onto the FRONT and write the verse opposite INSIDE!

MOTHER'S DAY

Instant Mother's Day Card

To dearest Mum,

I luv my Mother
Much more than my brother
He's really dumb
Not like my mum!

Lots of Love _____

How to Win
Noughts & Crosses

All you do is put 3 'O's or 3 'X's in a row on a nine-square grid. Not as easy as it sounds – *unless* you know the smart trick . . .

THE TRICK

- Imagine the black **O**s are your first three moves
- Fill them in – in any order
- You now have two possible ways to win
- On your fourth move, fill in *either* of the white ⓞs
- You've won!

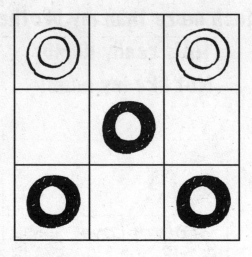

How to Win Noughts & Crosses

If your opponent goes first and blocks one of these positions, try another plan of attack:

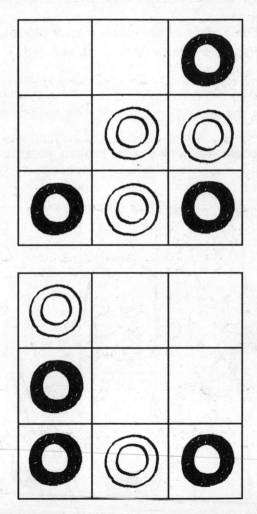

Broken Nose Trick

If your nose runs and your feet smell, what's wrong with you? You're built upside down! Talking of noses, here's a really yucky trick to make your relatives wince ...

1. Hide a piece of raw pasta in your mouth.
2. Hold your nose with your thumb and forefinger.
3. Bite the pasta so it makes a crunchy sound.
4. At the same moment, pull your nose to one side.
5. People will think you've 'broken' your nose!

How to Play Paper & Comb

Want to make music? But you don't have a musical instrument? No problem with this old trick!

- Take an ordinary pocket COMB

- Fold a piece of strong TISSUE paper around it

- Hold it against your slightly parted LIPS

- HUM whatever tunes you like!

Practical Parent-Speak

What ARE your parents talking about? They never seem to say what they actually mean, do they? Here's a smart guide to what they're really saying ...

But not in my lifetime!

100 miles to go!

I was a pain in the neck too!

That's MY job!

Practical Parent-Speak

No it doesn't!

You'll forget it by then.

I'm lying – it's agony!

It's the next 13 years that's the problem!

Perilous Pirates

Fancy the Pirate life? Sailing the Seven Seas, attacking ships full of Spanish gold, burying treasure on moonlit desert islands? It wasn't like that at all ...

RUM FACTS

Pirates didn't make prisoners walk the PLANK – they kept them for ransom or threw them overboard!

Most pirate FLAGS were plain black. They were raised just before they boarded another ship!

Some pirates did have their own flags with skulls and bones and cutlasses on them to help you see who was attacking you.

Pirates rarely buried TREASURE on desert Islands. They were too busy spending it!

Some pirates retired and wrote down the story of their life – these memoirs were bestsellers.

Perilous Pirates

CODE OF CONDUCT

We often think of pirates as dangerous folk who always broke the law. In fact they had strict rules designed to help them share out their booty, behave properly towards each other and avoid boredom: sounds like school!

1. You must do what you are told.

2. The Captain gets one and a half share of all booty.

3. The Master, Bosun, Carpenter and Gunner get one and a quarter share.

4. Anyone caught stealing will have their noses slit or be marooned on a deserted island.

5. Anyone caught trying to run away will be marooned.

6. Anyone caught hitting another pirate will be whipped 39 times.

7. All lights and candles (very risky on a ship) to be put out by 8 o'clock.

8. Musicians will play every day — except Sunday.

How to Remember Planets

What do you call crazy spacemen? Astro-nuts! But not as nutty as this way to remember the planets – from the nearest to the sun to the furthest away!

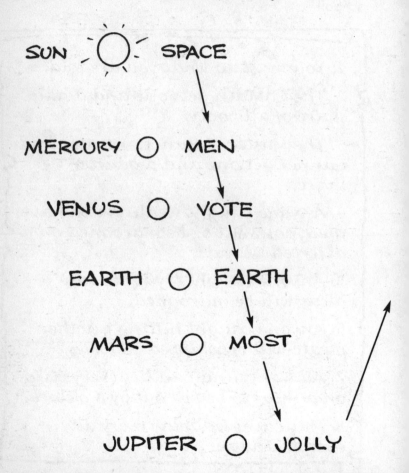

SUN · SPACE

MERCURY · MEN

VENUS · VOTE

EARTH · EARTH

MARS · MOST

JUPITER · JOLLY

How to Remember Planets

SATURN ○ OF THE SOLAR

URANUS ○ UNIVERSE'S

NEPTUNE ○ NINE

PLUTO ○ PLANETS

Perfect Playing Cards

Never play cards in the Jungle – it's full of
cheetahs! But when you ARE playing cards,
here's a real chance to be SMART ...

No one knows who invented cards –
probably the Chinese or Egyptians over a
1000 years ago.

There used to be 32 cards in a pack. The
52-card pack has only been used in the last
few centuries.

Some people think playing cards represent
the Calendar:

52 cards = 52 weeks in a year
4 suits = 4 seasons in a year
Red and Black = Night and Day

On English cards the kings, queens
and knights are from
the court of King HENRY VII.
The queens are based on Henry's wife,
ELIZABETH OF YORK.

The Queen of Spades always looks to
her LEFT. The other three queens look
to their RIGHT.

Perfect Playing Cards

Perfect Playing Cards

There is a museum just for playing cards in Stuttgart, Germany.

One of the best card-throwers in the world is American magician Ricky Jay.

Many magicians say the best card manipulator was CARDINI (real name was William Pitchford)!

The sharpshooter Annie Oakley could hit the thin edge of a playing card with a bullet at 30 paces!

Instant Poetry

Need to write a poem in a hurry? No problem! Just write these eight lines down in ANY ORDER and you've got a classic!

The tears glisten on my cheek

The stormy clouds have sprung a leak

Shall I compare you to a Summer's Day

Tis better to have loved and lost

The world's great Age begins anew

Close to the sun in lonely lands

The last red leaf is whirled away

Blest be the man that spares these stones

Rude Replies

You know how you always think of a smart reply ten minutes too late? Now you can have them on the tip of your tongue!

Rude Replies

HOW OLD ARE YOU?

I'M NOT OLD - I'M NEARLY NEW!

WHAT DOES BC STAND FOR?

BEFORE CALCULATORS

DIDN'T YOU HEAR ME CALLING YOU?

YES- BUT YOU TOLD ME NEVER TO ANSWER BACK!

WERE YOU COPYING JENNY'S SUMS?

I WAS JUST CHECKING SHE'S GOT HERS RIGHT!

Rotten Riddles

Riddles are a really cool way to show how smart you are – or how stupid other people are! But make sure you learn the answers!

① WHAT HAPPENS EVERY YEAR IN LAPLAND AT 10·30 ON NOVEMBER 31st ?

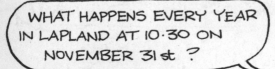

② I'VE GOT SEVEN FRIENDS, AND TWO-THIRDS OF THEM ARE GIRLS. HOW COME ?

③ MY DAD WENT THROUGH 3 RED LIGHTS IN FRONT OF A TRAFFIC COP – BUT THE COP DID NOTHING. HOW COME ?

④ THERE WERE 2 PLUMBERS, ONE WAS THE OTHER'S SON. THE OTHER ONE WAS NOT HIS DAD. HOW COME ?

Rotten Riddles

⑤ A MAN FLYING HIS PLANE OFF THE WEST COAST OF SCOTLAND DROPS A BAG OF FEATHERS AND A BAG OF COAL. WHICH HITS THE GROUND FIRST?

⑥

WHY DO MORE AMERICAN WOMEN DRIVE CARS THAN BRITISH WOMEN?

ANSWERS

1. Nothing! There are only 30 days in November!
2. The other one-third are GIRLS too!
3. My dad was WALKING!
4. The two plumbers were MOTHER and SON.
5. Neither – he was flying over the SEA!
6. Because there are a lot MORE women in America.

Raving Romans

Why did the Romans build such straight roads? So the Britons couldn't hide round the corner (or to stop their soldiers going round the bend)! Actually, they built 85,000 km of roads!

Roman kids played with marbles, rolled hoops and threw knucklebones!

Emperor Caligula drank pearls dissolved in vinegar!

The Romans had 3 words for kissing:

basium for people you've just met,

osculum for close friends and

suavium for your boy- or girlfriend!

Raving Romans

Two Roman postcards have been found in
England: an invitation to a birthday party,
and a cold soldier asking for more socks
and underwear!

Roman baker Eurysaces was buried in a
tomb shaped like an enormous oven!

Romans thought asparagus relieved bee-
stings and toothache.

They used powdered mouse brains as
toothpaste!

Raving Romans

If you met some Roman kids, you'd be able to play lots of games with them. They played hide and seek, hopscotch, leapfrog, chase and ball games. They had swings, kites, building blocks and dolls.

The Roman Emperor Caligula once made his horse a consul. He did lots of other crazy things like making it a crime to look down on his head (he was very sensitive about going bald).

Raving Romans

Romans were famous for their incredible parties.
They liked to show off their wealth and eat exotic
things like snails, swans, horses, peacocks and
flamingo tongues.

Romans ate so many flamingo tongues that
hunting flamingos was banned.

Albinus once ate 300 figs, 100 peaches and 10
melons as part of a single meal!

At some feasts there was a special room
called a *vomitorium* where guests could
be sick and then come back for seconds ...
and thirds ... and fourths!

How to Read School Reports

The dreaded moment: when your parents open your school report. But what does it REALLY mean? Here's a smart guide!

Shows Initiative . . .

(Cheats)

Always pleased to see him . . .

(Rarely turns up)

Takes an interest in the wider world . . .

(Stares out of the window all day)

Happy to work unsupervised . . .

(Never turns up)

How to Read School Reports

Prefers her own company . . .

(Smells terrible)

Lively contribution to classroom debates . . .

(Argues about everything)

Not afraid to tackle new subjects . . .

(Picks fights with new kids)

Keen sense of humour . . .

(Puts drawing pins on chairs)

Skilful Scooters

Scooters seem so modern, but actually the first one was invented in 1816 — nearly 200 years ago (even your dad had one!).

The scooter craze took off in the 1950s but faded away when skateboards arrived.

The scooter kicked back into fashion in the 1990s with the arrival of 'The Micro'.

The Micro was designed by Wim Ouboter — an inventor from Switzerland.

Celebrity scooterers include Robbie Williams, Gail Porter and Prince Harry.

Outside Europe, the Micro is known as 'The Razor'.

The first petrol-powered scooter was the 'Go-Ped'.

Other types of scooter are: the Skoooch, the E Shock, the Kickboard and the Rock Voxa!

The Kickboard has a joystick instead of handles.

Scooter tricks have brilliant names — have you tried the Crouch, the Bonus, the Ollie, the Endo or the Grind?!

There's even a scooter movie — *The Return of the Pedi!*

Skilful Scooters

Sizzling Simpsons

Doh! It's that crazy family again – the longest running cartoon series currently on TV. But what else?

The *Simpsons* started in 1987 as 30-second cartoons on the *Tracy Ullman Show* in America.

The Simpsons was created by Matt Groening, who named the main characters after his family. His dad and son are called Homer, his mum is Margaret and his sisters are Lisa and Maggie.

Homer's full name is Homer J. Simpson.
The 'J' stands for 'Jay'!

They live at 714 Evergreen Terrace, Springfield.
No one knows where Springfield is meant to be!

There are 90 characters in the show but only
11 people do the voices!

Sizzling Simpsons

Homer is voiced by Nancy Cartwright – a woman! She also voices Nelson!

Guests on the show include Paul McCartney, Michael Jackson, Neil Armstrong, Mr Spock, Sting and Britney Spears.

Bart Simpson often writes messages on the school blackboard, such as:

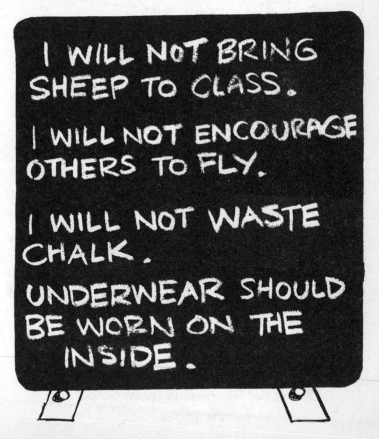

I WILL NOT BRING SHEEP TO CLASS.

I WILL NOT ENCOURAGE OTHERS TO FLY.

I WILL NOT WASTE CHALK.

UNDERWEAR SHOULD BE WORN ON THE INSIDE.

Skilful Skateboarding

How does a cat sound on a skateboard?
M-I-I-I-A-A-A-O-O-W-W! Skateboards have gone from
a craze to a sport in under 50 years!

Skateboarding was INVENTED in the 1950s by
Bill Richards and his son Mark, who ran a surfing
shop in Dana Point, California.

They realised that surfboarders wanted
something to do when the ocean was FLAT
and had no waves to surf on.

In 1957 they cut a ROLLER SKATE in half, and
put each half on the end of a mini surfboard —
the skateboard was born!

The first skateboard CONTEST was held in
1963 at the Pier Avenue Junior School in
Hermosa.

Skilful Skateboarding

The first skateboard MOVIE was made in 1965.
It was called *Skater Dater*!

The first outdoor SKATEPARK was built in
Florida in 1976.

Jumping into the air on a skateboard was
invented in 1978 by Alan Gelfand. He called it
an 'OLLIE'!

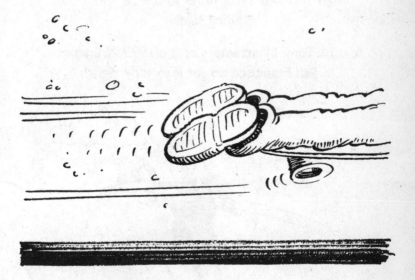

In 1990 Roger Hickey travelled 125.5 kph on a
skateboard, lying down – the FASTEST ever!

In 1999 Andy McDonald sped down a ramp and
jumped over 4 CARS – over 16 metres!

Skilful Skateboarding

The furthest distance travelled was by
Eleftherios Argiropoulos of Greece who
skateboarded 436.6 km. It took him 36 hours!

One of the world's top skateboarders is
American TONY HAWK.

Tony is the first person to achieve the '900' —
a trick where you speed down a ramp and
turn two and a half times in the air before
landing safely.

It took Tony 11 attempts at the 1999 X Games
in San Francisco to get it exactly right!

How to Attract Spiders

What do you buy a spider for Christmas? Four pairs of socks! But how do you get to know a spider in the first place?

- To make a spider come out and see you, hit an ordinary fork with long prongs on a surface to make it vibrate.

- Using the fork, touch the web very softly (so you don't damage it).

- A spider knows when something touches its web because wherever it is on the web, it feels it wobble or shake.

- The spider will almost certainly come and see if you're a big juicy fly!

Things That Are Something Else!

These are great little facts that are brilliant for 'Did you know ...' moments. For example, did you know ...

A cucumber is really a fruit!

Welsh rarebit is cheese on toast!

An English horn is actually an oboe from France!

A shooting star is not a star – it's a meteor!

A funny bone is not a bone at all!

Things That Are Something Else!

A pineapple in not a pine or an apple
— it's a large berry!

Turkish baths were invented by the
Romans!

A guinea pig is not from Guinea and
it's not a pig — it's a rodent from
South America.

A silkworm is actually a caterpillar!

A lead pencil is made of graphite, not
lead.

A firefly is not a fly — it's a beetle.

Special Spelling

Writers hav to bee very gud at speling! And sew doo smart kids!

HOW MANY LETTERS ARE THERE IN THE ALPHABET?

26?

NO, SILLY, 11! T-H-E-A-L-P-H-A-B-E-T

FACETIOUSLY HAS ALL THE VOWELS IN THE RIGHT ORDER!

Y'KNOW THE WORD CHRISTMAS? NOW SPELL IT!

C-H-R-I...

NO! 'IT' IS SPELLED I-T!

NO WORD IN ENGLISH RHYMES WITH ORANGE!

THERE ARE ONLY 12 LETTERS IN THE HAWAIIAN ALPHABET: A-E-H-I-K-L-M-N-O-P-U-W

Special Spelling

MUM, HOW DO YOU SPELL 'ARRY POTTER?

DO YOU MEAN HARRY?

NO, I'VE WRITTEN THE 'H' ALREADY

SPELL CONTENTMENT IN 4 LETTERS — A-P-N-S

CAN YOU SPELL BANANA?

I CAN START, BUT I DON'T KNOW WHEN TO STOP! BANANANANA NANANANANA NA...

HOW DO YOU SPELL 'RAIN'?

R-A-N-E

WHAT AN AWFUL SPELL OF RAIN

Special Spelling

THE WORD N-E-W-S WAS MADE FROM THE 4 POINTS OF THE COMPASS: NORTH, EAST, WEST, SOUTH.

HOW DO YOU SPELL CAT?

C-A-T

NO, YOU SPELL IT M-O-Q

HOW COME?

THE RAILWAY STATION WITH THE LONGEST NAME IN THE WORLD IS IN NORTH WALES. IT IS:

LLANFAIRPWLLGWYNGYLLGOGORYCHWYRNDRO-BWLLLLANTYSILIOGOGOCH

THE NAME PLATE IS NEARLY 24m LONG!

Special Spelling

The POLICE use special words to SPELL OUT words over their radios so no one makes a mistake.

A	ALPHA	N	NOVEMBER
B	BRAVO	O	OSCAR
C	CHARLIE	P	PAPA
D	DELTA	Q	QUEBEC
E	ECHO	R	ROMEO
F	FOXTROT	S	SIERRA
G	GOLF	T	TANGO
H	HOTEL	U	UNIFORM
I	INDIA	V	VICTOR
J	JULIET	W	WHISKY
K	KILO	X	X-RAY
L	LIMA	Y	YANKEE
M	MIKE	Z	ZULU

Stupendous Star Wars

What do you call a glass robot? See-Through PO! The *Star Wars* saga is one of the most successful sci-fi series ever. But did you know ...

STAR WARS was created by American director George Lucas.

JEDI Knights are a band of warriors with supernatural powers that come from 'the Force'.

Lucas' first film was called *THX-1138*. This number pops up in the *Star Wars* movies in all sorts of places!

Lucas' original name for Luke Skywalker was Luke Skykiller.

The Phantom Menace is the fourth *Star Wars* film made, but the first film in the saga!

Darth Vader's body was played by actor David Prowse, who was also the Green Cross man!

Stupendous Star Wars

Darth Vader's scary voice belonged to American actor James Earl Jones.

Robots CP30 and R2D2 were played by Anthony Daniels and Kenny Baker.

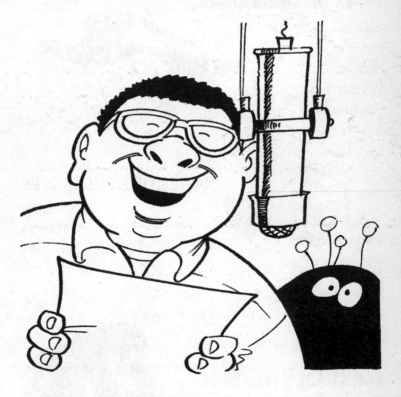

Hans Solo's ship was called *The Millennium Falcon*.

In the credits of *The Phantom Menace*, it says that Jabba the Hut was played 'by himself'!

Smart Sunglasses

At school, our teacher had to wear sunglasses because we were so BRIGHT! Sunglasses are smart because they look great AND they protect your eyes from the sun's ultraviolet rays!

TYPES OF SUNGLASSES

Polaroid
Reactive
Mirror
Wraparound
Compound
Aviators

NAMES OF SUNGLASSES

Shades
Mirrors
Face Furniture

TOP SHADES WEARERS

David Beckham
Bruce Willis
Ali G
Jackie Onassis

All About Superman

'Is it a bird? Is it a plane? No, it's Superman!' The Man of Steel with his pants on the outside is a top topic for smart kids.

Superman was invented by teenagers: Jerry Siegel and Joe Schuster.

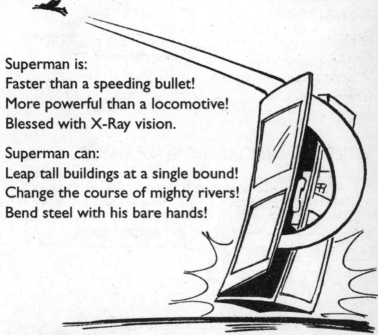

Superman is:
Faster than a speeding bullet!
More powerful than a locomotive!
Blessed with X-Ray vision.

Superman can:
Leap tall buildings at a single bound!
Change the course of mighty rivers!
Bend steel with his bare hands!

Superman was born on Planet Krypton and sent to Earth as a baby!

His chief enemy is Lex Luthor.

When he rushes into a phone box to change from mild Clark Kent into Superman, he puts his clothes in an invisible pocket on his belt!

Truth About Teachers

Teachers are very strange creatures. We spend 15 years of our lives with them, but we know so little about them. At last, your questions are answered!

WHY ARE THEY SO MISERABLE?

YOU FINISH SCHOOL AT 16 OR 18. TEACHERS GO TO SCHOOL FOR EVER! WOULDN'T YOU BE MISERABLE?

WHERE DO THEY GO IN THE HOLIDAYS?

TEACHERS COME FROM THE SAME FAMILY AS VAMPIRES.

SO IN THE HOLIDAYS THEY HANG UPSIDE DOWN IN A VERY DARK CAVE.

WHY DO THEY DRESS SO BADLY?

TEACHERS HAVE NO REFLECTION SO THEY CAN'T SEE THEIR CLOTHES DON'T MATCH.

Truth About Teachers

ARE TEACHERS CLEVER?

NO, IN 10 YEARS YOU'LL KNOW MORE THAN YOU DO NOW, BUT YOUR TEACHER WON'T KNOW ANYTHING NEW!

WHY DON'T TEACHERS EAT THE SAME FOOD AS YOU?

THEY MAY NOT BE CLEVER, BUT THEY'RE NOT STUPID!

WHERE DO THEY GO WHEN THEY RETIRE?

ON TRAINING DAYS TEACHERS GO TO STONEHENGE TO FEAST ON THE BODIES OF RETIRED TEACHERS

Talented Texting

Texting is a great way to send quick messages — and you don't need a mobile phone! Once you've learned the basics, you can write notes for anyone!

AFAIK	as far as I know
ASAP	as soon as possible
BCNU	be seeing you
B4	before
BFN	bye for now
BTDT	been there done that
BTW	by the way
CMB	call me back
CUL8R	see you later
F2F	face to face
GR8	great
HAND	have a nice day
IDK	I don t know
IU2U	it s up to you
LMK	let me know
Luv	love
MYOB	mind your own business
Msg	message
M8	mate
NAGI	not a good idea
NE1	anyone
N1!	nice one!
OIC	oh I see
Pls	please
RUOK	are you OK?
Sum1	someone
TA4N	that s all for now
THNQ	thank you
Wan2	want to
W/	with
Wknd	weekend
W8	wait
Ya	you
1daf1	wonderful
2day	today

Talented Texting

A picture's worth a thousand words! Especially when you're texting and it would take you four days to text a thousand words!

:-)	happy
:-(	sad
:-X	kiss
...(:)-]]	scuba diver
	owl
&-)	Harry Potter
(>:<)	Kenny
(@ @)	very tired
d:-)	baseball cap
#:-(	bad hair day
(I)	burger
o-%	scooter
(.V.)	elephant
!:o	Tintin
mmmm:===	crocodile

Instant Thank You Letter

Smart kids send Thank You letters. For one thing it's a nice thing to do – and the older your relative, the nicer they think you are!

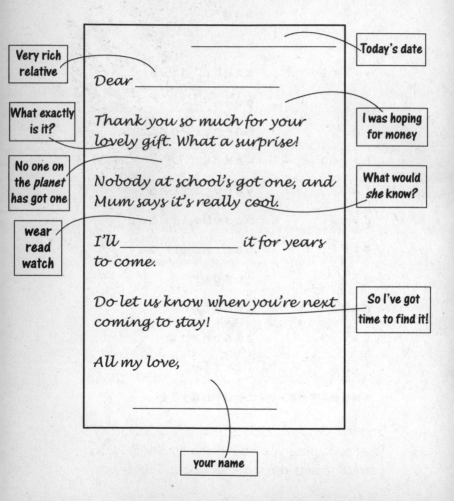

Very rich relative

Today's date

Dear _____

Thank you so much for your lovely gift. What a surprise!

What exactly is it?

I was hoping for money

Nobody at school's got one, and Mum says it's really cool.

No one on the *planet* has got one

What would she know?

I'll _____ it for years to come.

wear read watch

Do let us know when you're next coming to stay!

So I've got time to find it!

All my love,

_____

your name

Thrilling Thunder

What's the difference between a thunderstorm and a lion with toothache? One pours with rain, the other roars with pain! But how can you tell how far away the thunderstorm is?

When lightning flashes, you see it almost immediately because light travels at about **300,000 km per SECOND**.

When thunder crashes, you don't hear it for a while because sound travels slower – about **0.34 km per SECOND**.

So next time you SEE lightning flash, count the seconds until you HEAR the lightning. Each second means the storm is about 340 m away.

All About Thunderbirds

5 ... 4 ... 3 ... 2 ... 1 ... Thunderbirds are ... really cool!
This TV puppet series about International Rescue has
been popular for 40 years. Here's a smart guide.

THUNDER FACTS

The rescue organisation is run by the Tracy
family from a secret island in the Pacific.

Jeff Tracy's sons use rockets, planes and
submarines – the THUNDERBIRDS – to rescue
people in danger.

SCOTT flies Thunderbird 1, a rocket that gets to
the rescue fast. VIRGIL's T-2 is a large plane that
carries pods of rescue equipment. ALAN pilots
T-3, a space rocket, and GORDON pilots T-4,
an atomic submarine.

Communications are run by JOHN from
Thunderbird 5, a space station.

All About Thunderbirds

DID YOU KNOW?

Thunderbirds was created by Gerry Anderson – his wife Sylvia was the voice of Lady Penelope.

He got the idea from the work his brother did in Search and Rescue during World War II.

Parker, Lady Penelope's chauffeur, was based on a waiter called Albert in a restaurant Gerry used.

The Tracy brothers are named after the first five Americans in space.

'Thunderbird' was the name of an air base in America near where Gerry's brother learnt to fly – the name stuck with him for 20 years!

F.A.B. – the Tracy call sign – is short for 'Fab!' which is what people in the 1960s said instead of 'cool' or 'wicked'!

Tiptop Tintin

Blistering Barnacles! It's that teenager again! Yes, Tintin continues to be enjoyed by kids of all ages. But who is he?

Tintin was created by a Belgian cartoonist called Georges Remi in the 1930s.

Tintin is a teenage reporter and amateur detective who gets involved in thrilling adventures.

Remi took his initials 'G.R.', reversed them and called himself Hergé (which is how Belgians pronounce 'R.G.').

Tintin is famous for his quiff hairstyle and his dog Snowy.

Tintin and friends have tracked yetis in Tibet, flown to the moon, searched the seabed, fought with pirates and smugglers, and much more ...

Tiptop Tintin

Tintin's friends include Captain Haddock,
Professor Calculus and the twin policemen
Thompson and Thomson.

Captain Haddock is a bad-tempered sea
captain who drinks too much and says things
like 'Bachi Bazouks!'

Professor Calculus is an absent-minded
scientist and inventor with a hearing problem!
In France, Snowy is called Milou, and the twin
policemen are called Dupont and Dupond.

In Germany, Tintin is called 'Tim'!

Terrific Toys & Games

I once got an unbreakable toy for Christmas — so I broke all my other toys with it!

A RUBIKS CUBE has
43, 252, 003, 274, 489, 856, 000
possible positions.

The American version of
ACTION MAN is called
G.I. JOE.

LEGO is from the Danish
'leg godt' meaning 'play well'.

SCRABBLE was originally
called 'Criss Cross'.

Terrific Toys & Games

FRISBEES were originally
called PLUTO PLATTERS.

TEDDY BEARS were named after
U.S. President 'Teddy' Roosevelt!

TRIVIAL PURSUIT took its three Canadian
devisers 45 minutes to invent and 4 years to sell!

The YO-YO is based on a weapon
used by 16th-century Filipino hunters.

The WALKMAN was apparently
thought up by the head of Sony
while he was playing tennis.

Top Trainers

What runs around all day and lies at night with its tongue hanging out? A trainer! Remember, it's not who made them, it's how you wear them!

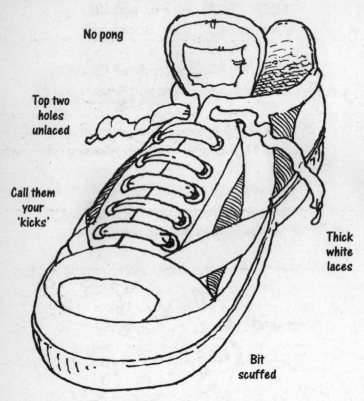

No pong

Top two holes unlaced

Call them your 'kicks'

Thick white laces

Bit scuffed

SNEAKY FACTS

NIKE was the Greek goddess of Victory!

ADIDAS is named after the founder **AD**olf **DAS**sler.

REEBOK is a South African antelope.

Top Trainers

TREAT YOUR FEET

The foot contains 26 bones, 33 joints, 107 ligaments and 19 muscles.

A quarter of your bones are in your feet, so look after them! When these bones are out of whack, so is the rest of the body. If your feet are healthy, the chances are you are too!

Walking is the best exercise for your feet.

There are 125,000 sweat glands in each foot. Your feet can sweat as much as a half-pint of moisture a day.

The average person takes 8,000 to 10,000 steps a day, which is about 115,000 miles over a lifetime. That's like walking around the world four times.

Top Tricks

You don't need equipment for these tricks – just a big smile and a smart brain!

YOU: Which of these two sentences is right? 'An egg yolk *is* white' or 'An egg yolk *are* white'?

THEM: 'An egg yolk *is* white.'

YOU: Wrong! An egg yolk is *yellow*!

YOU: Bet you can't put your right hand where your left hand can't reach it! (Just put your right hand under your left elbow!)

YOU: Guess what! I've got 11 fingers.

THEM: Rubbish!

YOU: On this hand I've got 1, 2, 3, 4, 5 (you count them off) and on my other hand I've got 10, 9, 8, 7, 6 (you count them off). 5 and 6 makes 11!

YOU: Bet I can kick a ball a few yards, make it stop and then come back to me – without anyone or anything touching it.

THEM: Bet you can't.

(Just kick the ball straight up in the air!)

Top Tricks

YOU: Bet I can make you say '50'. What is 5 plus 5?
THEM: 10!
YOU: And what is 10 times 4?
THEM: 40!
YOU: See? I told you I could make you say '40'.
THEM: No – you said you could make me say '50'.
YOU: And you just DID!

YOU: How many hands am I holding out?
THEM: 2.
YOU: No, 4. There are 2 hands on my watch!

YOU: What does T-O spell?
THEM: To.
YOU: And what does T-O-O spell?
THEM: Too.
YOU: What does T-W-O spell?
THEM: Two.
YOU: And what's the second day of the week?
THEM: Tuesday.
YOU: No! The second day of the week is Monday!

How To Age Trees

Can you see how the tree trunk below is made up of rings?

The light rings show the bark the tree grew in the spring. The dark rings show the bark the tree grew in the late summer.

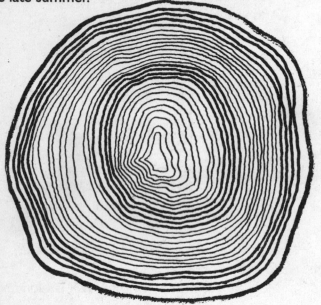

If you count up all the dark rings, the number you get is how many years the tree has been alive.

SMART FACT

Some Huon Pine trees in southern Tasmania are believed to be over 2,000 years old, making them one of the oldest living things in the world. But their roots are believed to be as much as 10,000 years old.